A **TRUE** BOOK™

Incredible Plants!

Crazy Plants

Karina Hamalainen

Children's Press®
An Imprint of Scholastic Inc.

Content Consultant
Michael Freeling, PhD
Professor
Department of Plant & Microbial Biology
University of California, Berkeley
Berkeley, California

Library of Congress Cataloging-in-Publication Data
Names: Hamalainen, Karina, author.
Title: Crazy plants / by Karina Hamalainen.
Description: New York, NY : Children's Press, an imprint of Scholastic Inc., 2020. | Series: A true book |
    Includes bibliographical references and index.
Identifiers: LCCN 2019004803 | ISBN 9780531234624 (library binding) | ISBN 9780531240052 (paper-
    back)
Subjects: LCSH: Plants—Adaptation—Juvenile literature.
Classification: LCC QK912 .H36 2020 | DDC 581.4—dc23
LC record available at https://lccn.loc.gov/2019004803

All rights reserved. Published in 2020 by Children's Press, an imprint of Scholastic Inc.
Printed in Heshan, China 62

Scholastic Inc., 557 Broadway, New York, NY 10012

2 3 4 5 6 7 8 9 10 R 29 28 27 26 25 24 23 22 21

**Front cover: Two kids inspecting
a stinking corpse lily**
Back cover: Venus flytrap

Find the Truth!

Everything you are about to read is true *except* for one of the sentences on this page.

Which one is **TRUE**?

T or F Some pitcher plants can eat animals as large as rodents.

T or F Rose plants are covered in thorns.

Find the answers in this book.

Contents

Jackal food plant

Venus flytrap

Think About It!

Look closely at the photo on these pages. What do you see in the image? How would you describe its appearance? Once you have made some observations about the organism in the image, think about why it looks the way it does. What benefits might come from its appearance? What evidence in the photo supports your explanation?

Intrigued?

Want to know more? Turn the page!

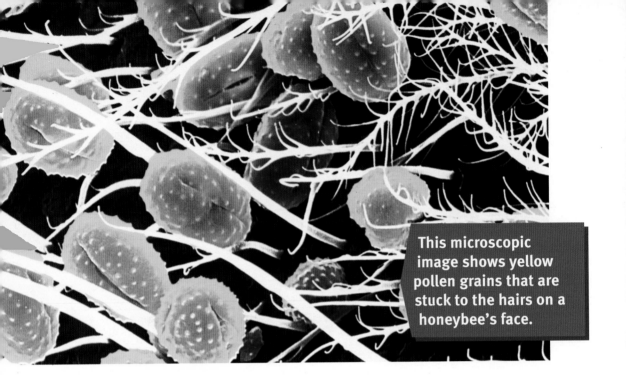

This microscopic image shows yellow pollen grains that are stuck to the hairs on a honeybee's face.

In Disguise

If you guessed that it is a flower that looks like a bee, then you are right! The plant is called a bee orchid. Bee orchids grow across Europe and the Middle East. The flower's disguise helps it reproduce.

To make new seeds, some plants need to share **pollen** with each other. Most flowers attract insects with bright colors and sweet nectar. But the bee orchid tricks them instead.

When real bees see the bee orchid, their instinct tells them there is a bee to mate with on the plant. When they land on the flowers, the real bees end up with clumps of pollen stuck to their bodies. When the insects move on, the pollen rubs off on other flowers. This allows the bee orchids to produce seeds and grow more plants.

Bee orchids are one of many crazy plants that have strange ways of meeting their needs. These unique **adaptations** help them grow and reproduce.

Pollen sticks to the entire body of a honeybee.

Bees and other animals help 30 percent of crops and 90 percent of wild plants reproduce.

California's redwoods grow taller than any other tree in the world.

Coast redwoods get 40 percent of their water from the fog that sweeps into the area regularly.

Extreme Adaptations

Plants need water, air, sunlight, and other nutrients to live. Differences in how much of each resource is available affect how plants live and grow.

Coast redwood trees thrive in Northern California's wet environment. While their roots soak up rainwater, their leaves capture water from fog. The trees get plenty of sunshine, too. As a result, many grow more than 300 feet (91.4 meters) high. They are the world's tallest trees!

Saguaro cacti are common sights in the deserts of the American Southwest.

It takes about 10 years for a saguaro cactus to grow 1 inch (2.5 cm) tall. In 100 years, it grows its first arm!

Thirsty Cacti

Deserts are areas where less than 10 inches (25.4 centimeters) of rain falls per year. Desert plants, such as cacti, have adaptations that help them save every last drop of water.

The saguaro cactus is one of the tallest cactus **species**. It can grow up to 60 feet (18.3 m) tall. Its roots are very shallow. They spread out in a circle as wide as the cactus is tall, so they soak up water from a large area.

Water Storage

A saguaro cactus stores water in its stem. The stem has accordion-like pleats that expand and contract to hold water. Other cacti, such as the brain cactus, have stems that fold. This creates ripples that trap water.

All cacti have spines, which are actually leaves. The cactus's pointy spines protect the plant and give it some shade from the sun. (Learn more about spines on page 37!)

The spines on these brain cacti are short and fine, making the plant look fuzzy.

Watery Worlds

Plants that live in the water will never go thirsty. At more than 5 feet (1.5 m) across, the Victoria water lily grows the largest pad-like leaves of any water plant. The enormous leaf pads soak up air and sunlight. The bigger the leaves, the more food the plant can make through **photosynthesis**.

Victoria water lilies can hold the weight of a child without sinking!

The underside of each Victoria lily leaf has prickles to prevent animals from eating it. Can you spot any prickles?

A baby hippopotamus sticks its head up through the water cabbage floating on the surface of the water.

Floating on Rivers

Water plants also have special adaptations to stay afloat. A Victoria lily pad has ridges on its underside that create air pockets under the pad. This keeps the leaves on the water's surface. Other water plants, such as the water cabbage, have leaves covered in superfine hairs that trap air bubbles that help them float.

It takes a Venus flytrap between 5 and 12 days to digest an insect.

This wasp flew too close to a Venus flytrap.

Very Unusual Nutrients

A fly catches the scent of sweet nectar. It lands on a red leaf and—SNAP! The fly is trapped as the leaves close around it. Over the next several days, the plant digests its meal. The soil in the wetland home of the Venus flytrap lacks important nutrients. The plant instead gets what it needs from insects. This may help explain the adaptation. The Venus flytrap is just one of many plants with unique sources of nutrients.

Fruit flies collect on the leaves of a butterwort.

Gotcha!

There are more than 600 known species of **carnivorous** plants. Like animal carnivores, these plants eat meat. All of these plants live in places with nutrient-poor soils. Over millions of years, they developed the ability to digest insects and other small animals. These creatures provide important nutrients that plants would otherwise get from the soil.

Most carnivorous plants use clever traps to catch their prey. Butterwort leaves are covered in sticky mucus, and insects become stuck in it. Then the plant injects **enzymes** that digest the insect right there on the leaf!

A sundew has trichomes, which are hairs sticking out of its leaves. Each trichome has a drop of sticky mucus on its tip. An insect struggles after becoming stuck, and the trichomes pull the leaves inward. They wrap around the prey, making escape impossible.

It can take up to 30 minutes for a sundew's leaf to curl around its prey.

A dragonfly is one of many insects that can become stuck in a sundew's mucus.

Pitcher Plants

All 100 species of pitcher plants have large leaves shaped like a jug with a lid. The lid produces nectar, which lures prey. Inside the jug is water and enzymes that digest food that falls in. Some pitcher plants are big enough to catch small rodents and amphibians.

Each species of pitcher plant has a unique shape. The California pitcher plant has a curved top. Insects are lured in and can't find their way out.

The giant Malaysian pitcher plant is the world's largest carnivorous plant. Its pitcher holds up to 1.6 gallons (6 liters) of fluid!

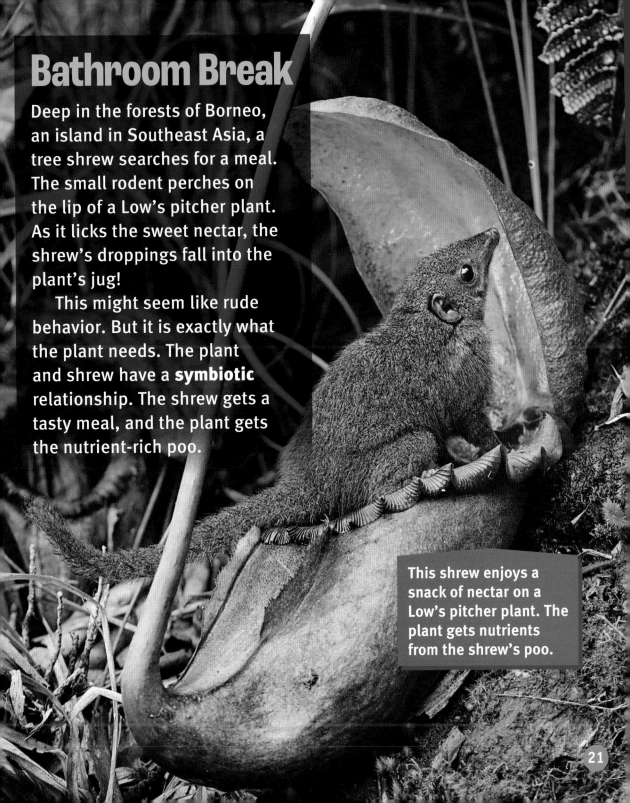

Bathroom Break

Deep in the forests of Borneo, an island in Southeast Asia, a tree shrew searches for a meal. The small rodent perches on the lip of a Low's pitcher plant. As it licks the sweet nectar, the shrew's droppings fall into the plant's jug!

This might seem like rude behavior. But it is exactly what the plant needs. The plant and shrew have a **symbiotic** relationship. The shrew gets a tasty meal, and the plant gets the nutrient-rich poo.

This shrew enjoys a snack of nectar on a Low's pitcher plant. The plant gets nutrients from the shrew's poo.

Up in the Air

In tropical forests, plants grow densely and must fight for sunlight. Some plants access light by growing high up in trees. These are called epiphytes (EP-uh-fites), or air plants. They get water from the rain and moist air. Epiphytes collect nutrients from debris that gathers around the point where they attach to the tree. Epiphytes do not harm the trees. This is why they are not **parasites**. Mistletoe, which sucks nutrients from its host tree until the tree dies, is a parasite.

Air plants called bromeliads cover a tree in Ecuador.

Hummingbirds pollinate most air plants.

Spanish moss does not harm the trees on which it grows.

Across the southeastern United States, you can see an air plant called Spanish moss. It drapes across tree branches. Though it looks like a moss, it actually is not. In fact, it's a relative of the pineapple.

Some orchid species are also epiphytes. One example is the ghost orchid. This white flower is one of the rarest orchids in the world.

A praying mantis climbs on a passionflower.

There are more than 400 species of passionflowers. Nine of them are native to the United States.

Screaming for Attention

The passionflower may look like an alien from another planet. It is, however, perfectly designed to get the attention of insects—especially butterflies. It has a brightly colored flower and an amazing fruity scent. Insects that come for the flower's nectar will surely spread its pollen to the next flower.

Passionflowers are one of many plants that have adaptations that attract insects and other animals that go on to help them reproduce.

Butterflies visit sweet-smelling plumeria blooms in search of nectar.

Sweet Scents

Different flowers' scents attract different **pollinators**. Some flowers, such as jasmine and lavender, have sweet scents that attract many kinds of pollinators. Birds, bees, and others creatures drink their nectar.

Other scents are tailored to specific animals. Plumeria flowers have a tiny center that hides nectar deep inside. Its scent attracts thrips, sphinx moths, and other creatures. Thrips are tiny insects that can crawl into the flower's throat. The sphinx moth reaches the nectar with its long **proboscis**, a type of mouth part.

The Perfect Pollinator

It's midnight, and the saguaro cactus flowers are in bloom. Their melon scent fills the air. A lesser long-nosed bat hovers close and reaches its long tongue into the nectar.

Pollen gets all over the bat's head as it eats. When the bat moves on to the next cactus, some of that pollen sticks to the plant, pollinating it. The saguaro cactus is one of more than 500 plant species that rely on bats to pollinate them.

A lesser long-nosed bat enjoys the nectar of a saguaro cactus bloom.

Bats help pollinate many fruits we eat, including bananas, mangoes, and peaches.

The Smell of Death

Some flowers might smell terrible to humans. But they smell like a tasty meal to the right pollinators! Here are a few extreme examples.

JACKAL FOOD PLANT
This African plant grows mostly underground. The only visible part is the flower, which takes a full year to grow. It produces a fruit that smells like poo. It is a favorite of jackals and birds!

ELEPHANT FOOT YAM
People eat the bulb-like structures that grow under this plant's stem. It's grown as a crop across Africa, Southeast Asia, and some Pacific Islands. Its flowers bloom for only about five days. During this time, their dead-animal smell attracts flies and beetles.

STINKING CORPSE LILY
With a diameter of 3 feet (.9m), the stinking corpse lily is the world's largest single flower. It is found in the tropical areas of Asia. As its name implies, it smells like a stinky corpse! This attracts flies.

CORPSE FLOWER
Asia's tropical corpse flower has the world's tallest flower structure. Its 10-foot-tall (3 m) flower spike has thousands of tiny flowers. These flowers only bloom for 12 to 48 hours every 4 to 10 years. Their dead-body scent attracts flies and beetles.

Some durian fruit can grow as large as a football!

Weird Fruits and Seeds

After a plant is pollinated, it produces seeds. Some seeds drop to the ground or float away on the wind. Others are in or on fruit. Animals eat the fruit and spread the seeds in their droppings.

Many fruits, such as apples and bananas, are sweet. But the durian tree's fruit smells like dirty socks and has a unique taste.

People either love it or hate it!

Fine $500

No durians

Eating durian on Singapore's mass transit system is not allowed because the fruit smells so bad.

Rambutan is named for the Malaysian word for hair.

Dragon fruit grow on cacti.

Fantastic Fruit

Much of the fruit you see in the grocery store is round and smooth. But there are many fruits with extreme shapes and textures. Star fruit, like its name says, is shaped like a star when sliced. Rambutan looks like a sea urchin, but the flesh inside is sweet and tastes like a grape. Dragon fruit is oval-shaped with pink skin and pointy flaps.

Super Seeds

Some seeds, such as those of orchid plants, are as small as a grain of dust. But the world's largest seed is the coconut of the coco de mer palm tree. A single coconut can weigh up to 40 pounds (18.1 kg). The coco de mer palm grows only in the Seychelles Islands in the Indian Ocean. If you ever visit, watch out for falling coconuts!

Coco de mer flowers are fertilized by lizards.

A boy balances a coco de mer coconut on his head.

The Rarest of the Rare

There are about 400,000 species of plants on earth. Scientists estimate that about one-third of them are endangered. This means they are at risk of becoming extinct, or disappearing completely. Many plants face the same threats: climate change, habitat destruction, invasive species, and people taking the plants from the wild to sell. Here are some of the most endangered plants on the planet.

Western Underground Orchid

This plant lives most of its life underground. Only the flowers peek through the soil when in bloom.

Population: About 50 plants

Location: Western Australia

Biggest threat: Habitat destruction

Poke-Me-Boy Tree

These spiny shrubs live in low-lying areas of only two islands in the British Virgin Islands.

Population: Unknown

Location: Caribbean

Biggest threat: Climate change and rising sea levels

Venda Cycad

This tree is often mistaken for a palm. It's actually a cycad, the oldest family of plants on earth.

Population: None in the wild; only known examples grown by humans

Location: South Africa

Biggest threat: Humans illegally taking the plants to use as decoration

Mount Diablo Buckwheat

This flowering herb was thought to be extinct until 2005, when one plant was found. Then in 2016, a large population was discovered.

Population: About 1.8 million plants

Location: Northern California

Biggest threat: Invasive species

Ascension Island Parsley Fern

This tiny fern was thought to be extinct until 2009, when scientists found four plants in the wild.

Population: About 40 plants

Location: Ascension Island, Atlantic Ocean

Biggest threat: Invasive species (goats) eating them

A ring-tailed lemur sits on the spiny branches of an octopus tree.

Verreaux's sifaka lemurs are one of the few animals that can avoid the ocotillo's spines and eat its leaves.

Defense Strategies

Watch your step if you visit the spiny forests in southwestern Madagascar off the coast of Africa. Many of the plants there have pointy spines, including Madagascar ocotillos and octopus trees. Spines are a type of modified leaf that protects the plant. Because most plants are stuck in one place, they have developed unique strategies—such as spines—to protect themselves from predators.

Pick Your Poison

Oleanders are beautiful . . . but deadly! The whole plant contains poisonous chemicals. They cause stomach pains, vomiting, heart problems, and eventually death in humans and animals. Animals don't eat them. The plants reproduce by fooling

The dangerous poison in castor bean seeds is called ricin.

bees hunting nectar into visiting their flowers, though there's no nectar to be found. Other plants have poison only in certain parts. For the castor bean plant, the poison is in its bean-like seeds. Don't eat the spooky-looking fruit of a doll's eye, either! These berries are the poisonous part of that plant.

BEWARE
OF
POISON IVY

Spotting Poison Ivy

Unless you're in California, Hawaii, or Alaska, you should keep an eye out for poison ivy when hiking in the United States. The poisonous oils on and in this plant cause an itchy rash. This discourages most animals from eating it, keeping the plant alive! Look out for plants that have clusters of three shiny leaves that sprout from a red stem. Poison ivy plants can be small shrubs or vines.

Here's how to prevent getting a rash when on a hike:
1. Avoid areas where you know poison ivy is.
2. Look out for shiny plants. Steer clear of them!
3. Wear long pants and sleeves.
4. If you think you have come in contact with poison ivy, shower immediately and wash your clothes.

This close-up photo shows the hairs on a stinging nettle.

Don't Touch!

Some plants can sting you if you touch them. One of the most painful plants to brush up against is the stinging nettle. It has specialized hairs with a bulb at the end. When the bulb is knocked off, the hairs inject a stinging fluid into the skin, like a shot you would get at the doctor's office. The fluid causes an itchy burning rash that can last up to 12 hours!

Making a Point

People say "every rose has its thorn," but that is incorrect! Thorns are pointy branches or stems. Many plants, such as acacia trees, have menacing thorns for protection. But roses actually have prickles. Prickles are parts of the plant's skin that stick out on the stem.

Unusual adaptations help plants in many different ways. But whether it is hairs for floating or prickles for protection, they all come down to the same basic need: survival!

A giraffe uses its tongue to carefully reach for leaves among a tree's thorns.

Design a Plant

In this activity, you will design a plant to survive the particular demands of its environment.

Directions

1 Pick one option from each section in the chart below to create the habitat your plant will live in.

Plant Habitat Characteristics

Climate	Tropical, Temperate, or Arctic
Temperature	Hot, Warm, or Cold
Rainfall	Rainy, Moderate, or Dry
Sunshine	Sunny or Shady

2 On a separate sheet of paper, describe your plant's habitat in a few sentences. Then think about what it would take to survive in these conditions. What adaptations will your plant need?

3 Consider what predators the plant may have. What beneficial relationships might it have with other plants or animals? Write a sentence or two about its relationship with other plants and animals.

4 Draw a picture of your plant. Add labels for its defenses or other adaptations to its habitat. Write a short paragraph about your plant's life cycle.

Explain It!

Look at the plant you invented. Flip back through the book and pick a few pages that helped you decide how to design your plant. What adaptations did you choose?

True Statistics

Approximate number of plant species known to science: 400,000

Approximate number of carnivorous plant species: 600

Approximate number of pitcher plant species: 100

Height of the tallest tree: 380 ft. (115.8 m); named Hyperion, a coast redwood

Diameter of the largest type of single flower: 3 ft. (0.9 m), the corpse flower

Age of the oldest coast redwood tree: More than 2,000 years old; named Helios

Weight of the largest type of seed: 40 lbs. (18.1 kg), the coco de mer coconut

Did you find the truth?

T Some pitcher plants can eat animals as large as rodents.

F Rose plants are covered in thorns.

Resources

Other books in this series:

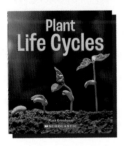

You can also look at:

Duke, Shirley Smith. *Step-by-Step Experiments With Plants*. Mankato, MN: Childs World, 2012.

Hirsch, Rebecca E. *When Plants Attack: Strange and Terrifying Plants*. Minneapolis: Millbrook Press, 2019.

Probst, Jeff. *Remarkable Plants*. New York: Puffin Books, 2017.

Silvey, Anita. *The Plant Hunters: True Stories of Their Daring Adventures to the Far Corners of the Earth*. New York: Farrar Straus Giroux, 2012.

Glossary

adaptations (ad-ap-TAY-shunz) changes in an organism or its parts that make it more fit to live in its environment

carnivorous (kahr-NIV-ur-uhs) having meat as a regular part of the diet

enzymes (EN-zymz) substances produced by living organisms that cause specific chemical reactions

parasites (PAYR-uh-sites) organisms that live on or in another organism of a different species to obtain nutrients

photosynthesis (foh-toh-SIN-thuh-sus) the process in which carbon dioxide, sunlight, and water are converted into food for plants

pollen (PAH-luhn) the fertilizing particle of plants that consists of fine, powdery, yellowish grains

pollinators (PAH-luh-nay-turz) organisms that transfer pollen between plants for fertilization

proboscis (proh-BOS-kis) long mouth parts of an insect adapted for sucking or piercing

species (SPEE-sheez) one of the groups into which organisms are divided; members of the same species can mate and have offspring

symbiotic (sim-bee-AH-tik) an interdependent relationship between two organisms

Index

Page numbers in **bold** indicate illustrations.

About the Author

Karina Hamalainen has been a writer and editor of Scholastic's science and math magazines for 10 years. Today, she is the executive editor of *Scholastic MATH*, a magazine that connects current events to the math that students are learning in middle school. She's written five books and many articles about everything from the science of *Star Trek* to the effects of the *Deepwater Horizon* oil spill on the Gulf of Mexico. She lives in New York City, and tries to escape the city and explore the wilderness often!